A FRIEND TO
NATURE

LAURA KNOWLES   REBECCA GIBBON

WELBECK
EDITIONS

For Sam, who loves to race
through the park, and William,
who makes friends with the snails.
L. K.

For Jonny . . .
R. G.

Published in the USA in 2021 by Welbeck Editions

An imprint of Welbeck Children's Limited,
part of Welbeck Publishing Group.
20 Mortimer Street, London, W1T 3JW

ISBN 978 1 91351 920 9

Printed in Dongguan, China

10 9 8 7 6 5 4 3 2 1

Many thanks to consultant Caylin Gans,
practitioner and mentor in environmental education, nature, and
play-based pedagogies. Founder of Forestschooled.com

CONTENTS

A NOTE TO PARENTS AND EDUCATORS

If you've picked up this book, it's probably because you want the child or children in your life to spend more time outdoors and to connect more deeply with nature. It can feel like we all—children and adults alike—spend too much of our lives indoors and are losing touch with the natural world.

When children don't have the opportunity to connect with nature, they also miss out on a wonderful opportunity to nurture their independence, make risk judgements, recharge, reflect, and explore their own inner world and emotions. They don't get to build empathy for a natural world that needs our protection now more than ever. Scientific studies have shown that spending time in nature as a child has a positive impact on lifelong mental health*. It really is one of the best investments a child can make in their own future happiness.

We can often feel as though children need to take part in organized activities or sports in order to be kept stimulated, but the beauty of nature is that you don't need to do anything to reap the benefits. Allowing children time for unstructured play—and time just to be—is greatly valuable, too.

Another fantastic thing about nature is that you can even find it in urban areas if you search hard enough. Although it is wonderful if you can spend time in the country, connecting to nature isn't about finding an untouched wilderness. It's not all or nothing. The key is to take time to find it on your doorstep and to cherish what you find. I hope this book helps provide some ideas and inspiration for any family that wants to connect with and protect nature, no matter where they live.

*For more information, refer to the web links on page 72.

STAYING SAFE OUTDOORS

The natural world is a wonderful place to have fun, relax, explore, and develop your independence. But it can also be a dangerous place if we don't think through our actions and follow safety rules.

Always follow these rules to stay safe:

- Always make sure a grown-up is nearby, and don't wander out of sight.

- The grown-up decides how close you need to stick to them, depending on where you are.

- Be extra careful near ponds, rivers, lakes, and the ocean. Water can be dangerous and unpredictable.

- Never light a fire or use sharp tools without a grown-up's help.

- Never eat anything you find outdoors without checking with a grown-up first! Some things might look tasty but are in fact poisonous and can make you sick.

- Learn about the types of wildlife that live in the area you are exploring. If you live in an area that is also a habitat for any dangerous or poisonous animals, follow the local rules so that both you and the wildlife can stay safe.

- Wash your hands when you return home, especially before you eat.

Always prepare for the weather!

- If you're going somewhere that might be muddy or slippery, wear rubber boots or shoes with nonslip soles.

- Take a waterproof jacket to stay dry in case it rains.

- Don't forget to wear sunscreen. The sun can damage our skin, even on a cloudy day in the spring or summer.

- Don't forget to carry a bottle of water with you—exploring outside can make you thirsty, especially on a hot summer day.

THE FRIENDSHIP PLEDGE

This is my pledge, my promise, my vow,
lasting forever, starting now:
I'll be a friend to nature.

A good friend listens, a good friend cares,
isn't greedy, always shares,
and I'll be that friend to nature.

A good friend respects the other's needs,
gives them the time and space to breathe,
and I'll be that friend to nature.

A good friend speaks out when something is wrong,
doesn't give up when the journey is long,
and I'll be that friend to nature.

This is my pledge, my promise, my vow,
lasting forever, starting now:
I'll be a friend to nature.

8

GETTING TO KNOW NATURE

When we are friends with someone, we are interested in them. We like to spend time with them and find out all about their likes and dislikes. The better we get to know someone and the closer we become, the more we care about them and want them to be happy.

It is the same with nature: the more time we spend in the natural world and the more interest we take in it, the deeper we care about nature and want to look after it. So if we want to be a good friend to nature, let's start by getting to know it better . . .

SPEND TIME WITH THE TREES

It can be fun to run, shout, whirl, and laugh when outside.
But to really get to know nature, you must be quiet, be still—pretend
to be part of the earth, rocks, and trees. Open your eyes and your
ears and really *look* at what's around you.

The sounds of nature

If you visit the woods, a park, the countryside, or the
coast, play the quiet-as-a-mouse game. For a couple
of minutes, stay silent, don't move, and listen hard.
What sounds can you hear? Can you hear any sounds
you don't normally hear when you're indoors?

Nature noises

Bees buzzing	Branches creaking	Rain dripping
Water gurgling	Insects chirping	Frogs croaking
Wind whooshing	Twigs snapping	Birds singing

Can you hear any other nature noises?

Make friends with a tree

Find a tree near your home and give it a name. Look at its leaves, bark, and branches— is the tree the same as the other trees around it? Draw a picture of it or take a photo. Make bark and leaf rubbings with a crayon. Visit your tree friend throughout the year and look at whether it changes over time. Does it shed its leaves in the fall and flower in the spring?

Leaf hunt

Go on a leaf hunt and pick up any nice fallen leaves you find. Do you know what tree they came from? If you don't, try looking online or use a leaf identifier app to help.

Leaf pressing

Place your leaves between sheets of newspaper and carefully lay this between the pages of a heavy book. Pile more books or another heavy object on top. Keep the leaves like this for two or three weeks. When they're ready, glue your pressed leaves onto paper or use a needle and thread to string them together to make a decoration for your room.

"look deep into nature and then you will understand everything better."
Albert Einstein

Albert Einstein was a very smart scientist whom many people think of as a genius. What do you think he meant when he said this?

BUILD A BLIND TO GET CLOSER TO NATURE

The best way to get a better look at wildlife is to let it come closer to you while you stay hidden. Build a blind, step inside it, then watch and wait.

1. Find a place that has plenty of trees and fallen branches, such the woods or a local park with trees.

2. Gather lots of long, thin branches, taller than yourself.

3. Lean your branches up against a tree trunk. You'll need to find a forked trunk so the branches stay put.

4. Add more branches to cover up any gaps, and stuff twigs and leaves into the smaller gaps.

6. For extra comfort, put a blanket down inside your blind. Now peek out and see what wildlife comes to you!

Ask a grown-up to help build your blind and then check that it is safe and sturdy before you go inside it.

GET TO KNOW A FLOWER

Have you ever looked closely at a plant? Really closely?
Find a flower and see if you can spot all its different parts, which
are labeled below. Flowers come in all kinds of shapes, so some
parts might be easier to identify than others.

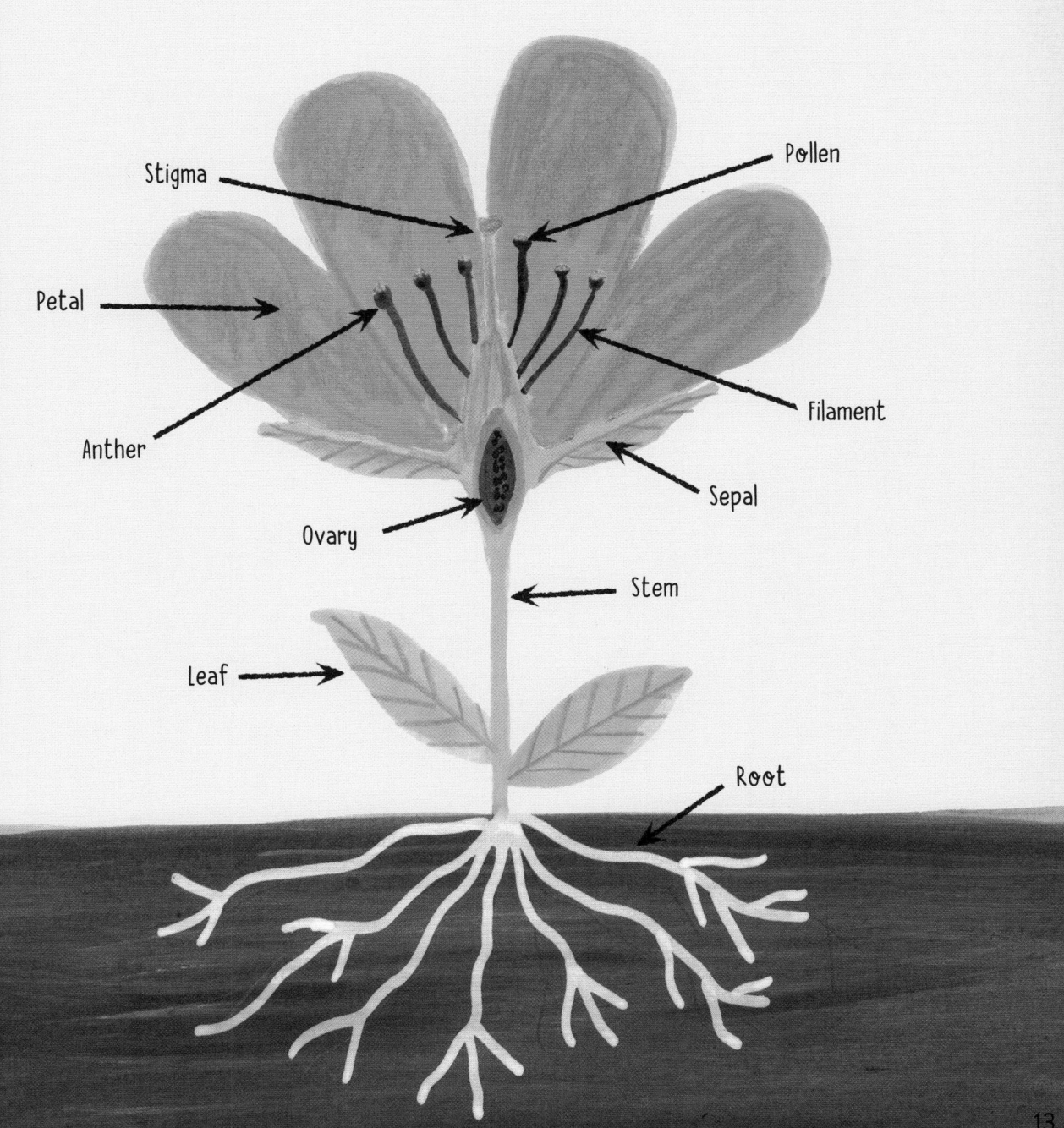

CREEPY-CRAWLY HUNT

Go on a creepy-crawly hunt! Creepy-crawlies are insects, spiders, slugs, snails, and tiny critters. Search in bushes and trees, under rocks and rotting logs—these creatures love to hide in dark and damp places.

Look for us!

Here are some creepy-crawlies you might spot on your hunt. There are different types of creatures in different parts of the world. Can you find any other kinds near your home?

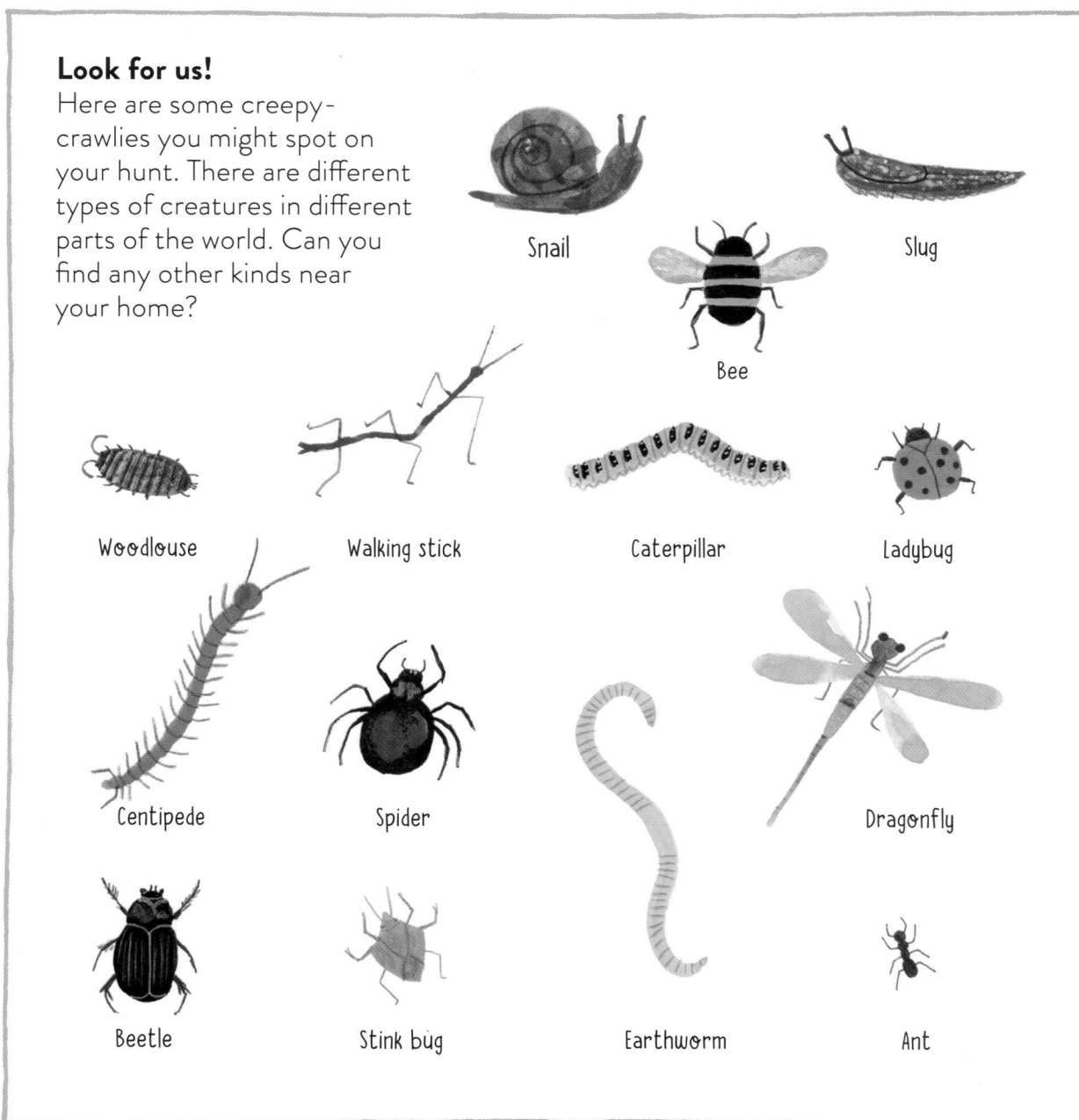

Snail

Slug

Bee

Woodlouse

Walking stick

Caterpillar

Ladybug

Centipede

Spider

Dragonfly

Beetle

Stink bug

Earthworm

Ant

Take a photo or
draw a picture of any
creepy-crawlies you
find, but leave the
little guys where
you find them.

Story walk
Go on a walk and make up a story about the things you
see. Everyone on the walk (including grown-ups) takes
turns making up a line of the story and saying it out
loud. Where will your imagination take you?

. . . It was scared of the
deep, dark forest, so it
stayed up high in an old
tree . . .

*"Once upon a time
there lived a timid
squirrel . . .*

. . . but this was no ordinary tree. It was
the oldest, biggest tree in the forest, and
that made it magical . . ."

THE LIFE CYCLE OF A BUTTERFLY

Over time, you will go through many changes as you grow into an adult. But that's nothing compared with the changes a caterpillar undergoes to grow into a beautiful butterfly!

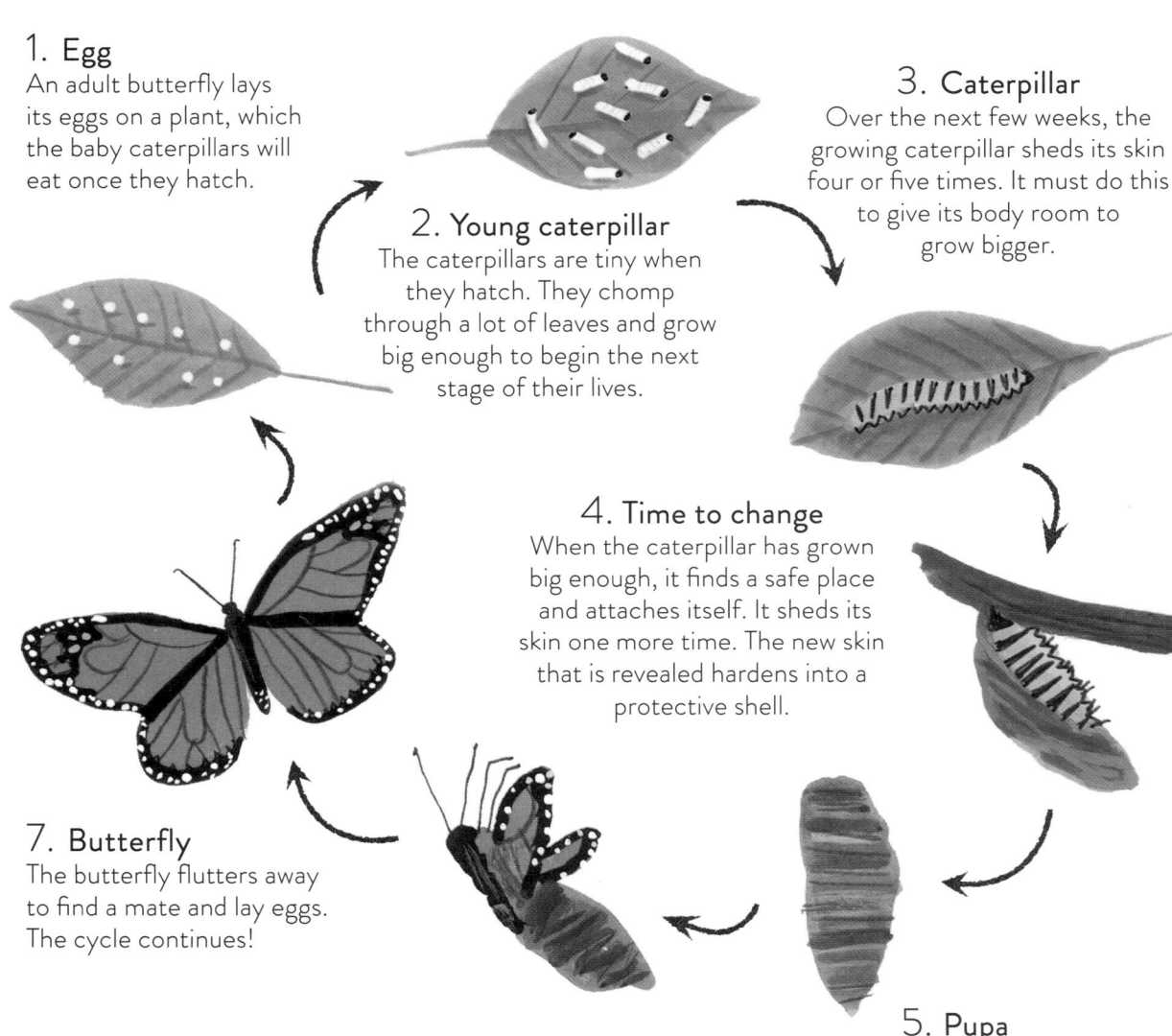

1. Egg
An adult butterfly lays its eggs on a plant, which the baby caterpillars will eat once they hatch.

2. Young caterpillar
The caterpillars are tiny when they hatch. They chomp through a lot of leaves and grow big enough to begin the next stage of their lives.

3. Caterpillar
Over the next few weeks, the growing caterpillar sheds its skin four or five times. It must do this to give its body room to grow bigger.

4. Time to change
When the caterpillar has grown big enough, it finds a safe place and attaches itself. It sheds its skin one more time. The new skin that is revealed hardens into a protective shell.

7. Butterfly
The butterfly flutters away to find a mate and lay eggs. The cycle continues!

6. Emerging butterfly
When the butterfly is fully formed, it breaks out of its chrysalis shell. Once it has emerged, it rests while its new body hardens. It pumps blood into its wings to stretch them out, ready to fly.

5. Pupa
The caterpillar is now called a pupa, or chrysalis. Inside its case, the pupa is going through major changes as it turns into a butterfly. This change is called metamorphosis.

PARTS OF A BUTTERFLY

Butterflies flutter by on warm days in the spring and summer.
They drink nectar from flowers, so a flower garden or a wildflower meadow
is the ideal place for them to feed—and the best place to spot them.

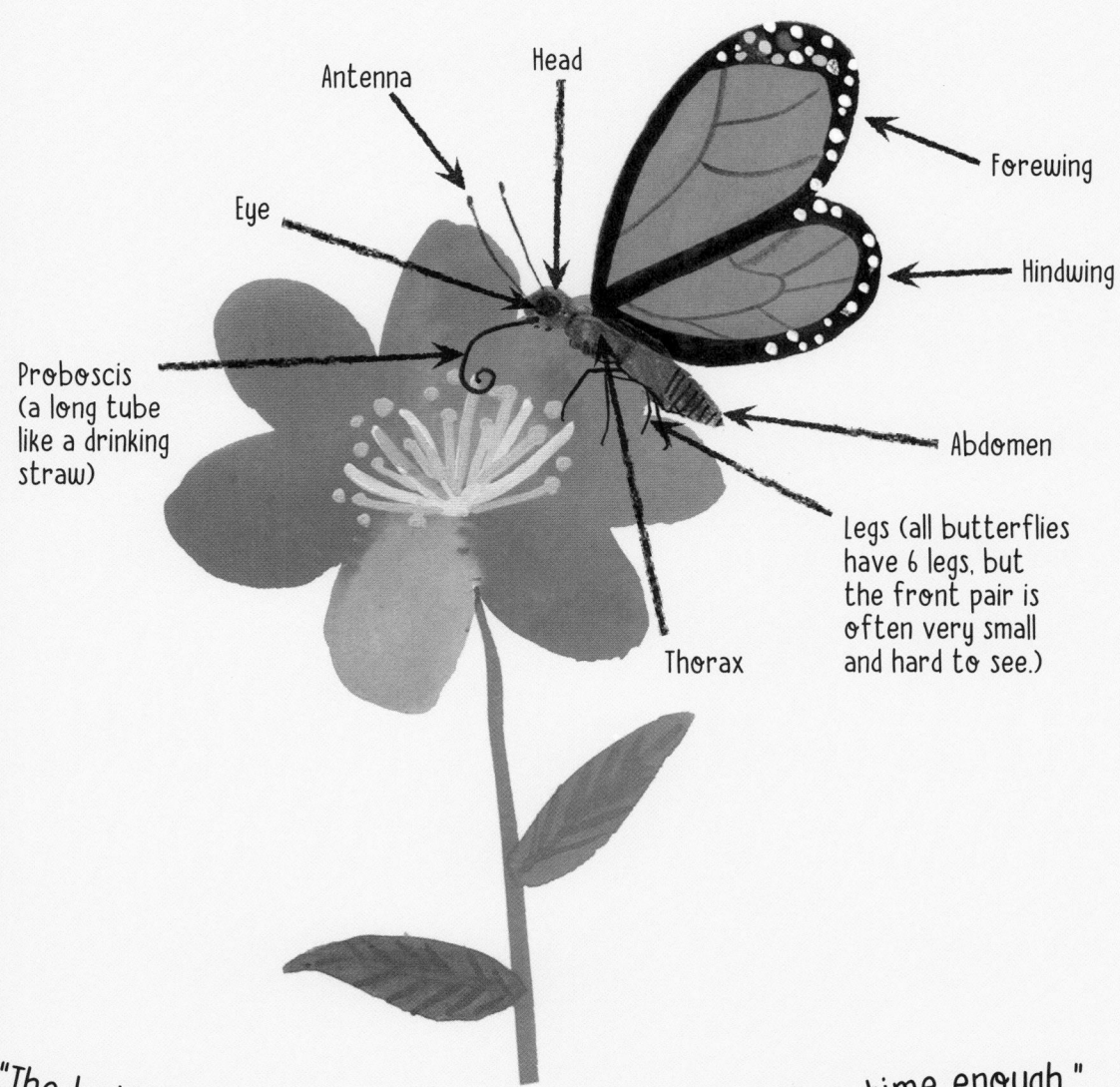

Antenna

Head

Forewing

Eye

Hindwing

Proboscis
(a long tube
like a drinking
straw)

Abdomen

Legs (all butterflies
have 6 legs, but
the front pair is
often very small
and hard to see.)

Thorax

"The butterfly counts not months but moments, and has time enough."

Rabindranath Tagore
Bengali poet and
Nobel Prize winner

SEE THE BIGGER WORLD

Getting to know nature better isn't just about paying attention to the little things around you, such as flowers and insects. It's also about realizing that you are part of something bigger. For example, the sky is immense. Have you ever noticed how passing clouds always change shape?

Cloud art

Lie down on a picnic blanket on the grass and look up at the cloudy sky. Are the clouds thin and hazy, or thick and puffy? How quickly are they drifting by? Try to spot clouds that are shaped like animals or other objects—maybe there's one that looks like a lion, a ship, or a dragon. Take turns finding cloud pictures. Can you guess the pictures your fellow cloud-spotters can see?

STARGAZING

On a clear night, look up at the sky and try to spot constellations—groups of stars that we join together with imaginary lines to make pictures. The constellations often have ancient stories. Can you make your own constellation and think up a story to go with it?

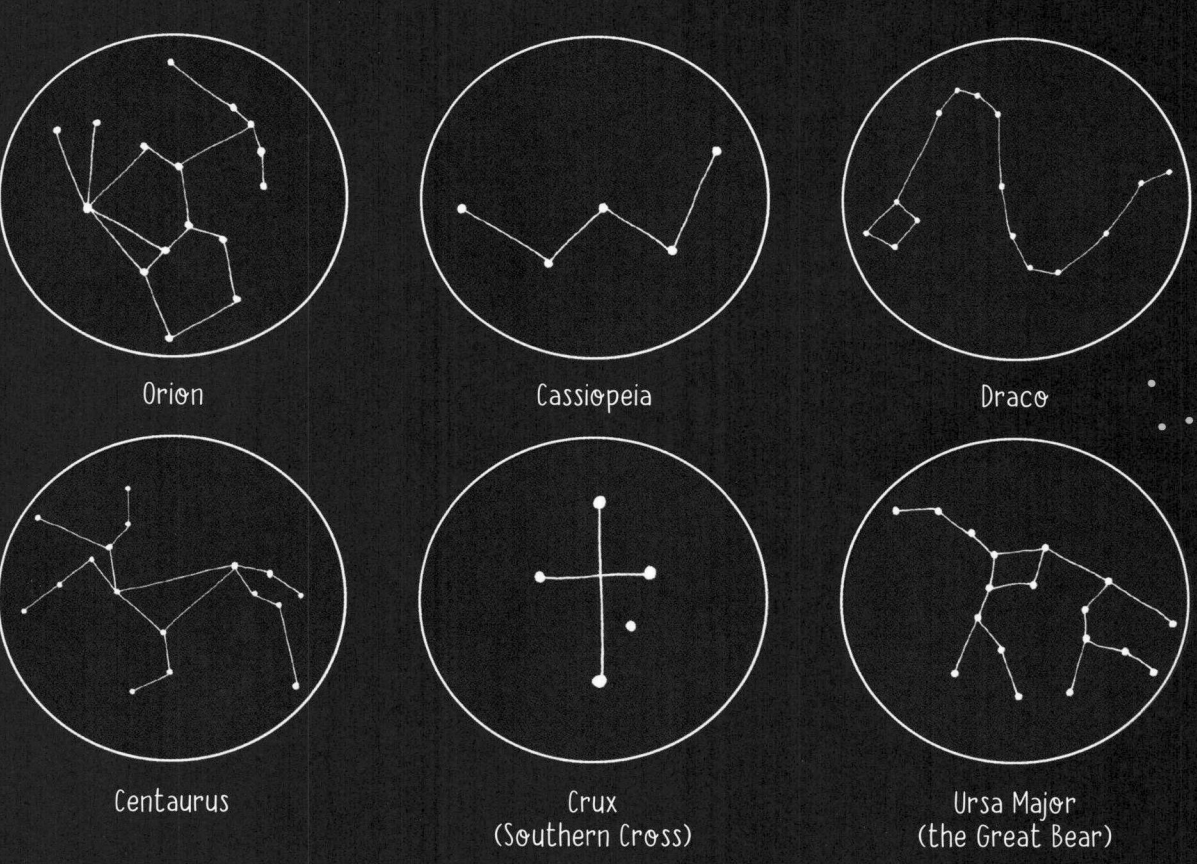

Orion

Cassiopeia

Draco

Centaurus

Crux
(Southern Cross)

Ursa Major
(the Great Bear)

Many of the stars that can be seen from Earth's northern half, or hemisphere, are different from those that can be seen from the southern half.

"We are made of star-stuff. Our bodies are made of star-stuff. There are pieces of star within us all."

Carl Sagan
American astronomer

MAKING A HOME FOR NATURE

You've been out exploring nature and getting to know it a little better. Maybe you've walked through winding woods or noticed birds soaring high in the sky. Why not invite nature closer to you? Whether you have your own backyard or a balcony—or maybe an outdoor space at your school—there are lots of ways you can make a home for nature.

INVITE WILDLIFE IN

Many animals are less likely to venture into a wide-open space because they are scared a predator might try to catch them. To create a place where wild animals feel safe to come and go, it's important to provide lots of secret holes and spaces for them to hide in.

Let it grow

What better way to invite wildlife into your backyard than by leaving the grass to grow long? So ask the grown-ups to leave a patch unmown! The long grass will soon become a home for lots of insects, which other animals will feed on. Alternatively, you can replace your grass with wildflowers or ground-cover plants. Ask at your local garden center for advice.

Build a bug hotel

Whatever the size of your yard, there's always room for a bug hotel! A tiny "beetle B and B" or a grand "creepy-crawly castle" will give insects a place to sleep through the winter or a safe spot to lay their eggs. You can make a small one that fits on a balcony, or ask your teacher if your class could help make one at school.

Nature doorways

Wildlife needs space. If a yard is surrounded by a solid fence, many animals will never be able to get in. Birds can fly over the fence, unlike frogs and toads, for example. You can help wildlife by asking an adult to make a doorway by sawing a small opening at the bottom of a wooden fence. A hole about 6 inches wide and tall will be big enough.

Don't forget to check that your neighbors are also happy to have a nature doorway!

You will need

- Bricks
- Waste pieces of lumber or old pallets
- Old tiles or asphalt roof shingles
- Bamboo cane (sawed into pieces)
- Straw
- Twigs
- Dry leaves
- Moss
- Bark
- Pine cones
- Corrugated cardboard
- Old clay flowerpots
- Soil
- Stones

1. Find a flat, even patch of ground to put your bug hotel, where it won't be disturbed (ask a grown-up for permission to use the space).

2. Lay some bricks on the ground to make the base of your hotel.

3. Place the wooden pallets on top of the bricks. If you are using individual pieces of wood, arrange them on the bricks. Then line more bricks along the edges to make walls.

4. Place another pallet on top of the walls and build another level. Add more levels to your hotel, until the bug hotel is no more than 3 feet tall, so that it still feels sturdy.

5. Stuff the other materials you've collected into the gaps of your bug hotel to create sheltered hiding places for different insects.

6. Place old tiles on top of your bug hotel. This will help keep your insects cozy and dry by keeping the rain out. Instead of tiles, you could use asphalt roof shingles securely attached so they won't blow away.

7. Finally, give your bug hotel a name! Make a little sign to go on your architectural masterpiece.

The great thing about making a bug hotel is you can use pretty much any materials you have handy. If you don't have some of the things listed here, try making them out of other materials instead.

FROG OR TOAD?

Can you tell the difference between a toad and a frog?
These two amphibians (*am-FIB-ee-ans*) might seem alike, but they
are different! Depending on where you live, you might come across
different kinds of toads or frogs. Learn how to tell which is which!

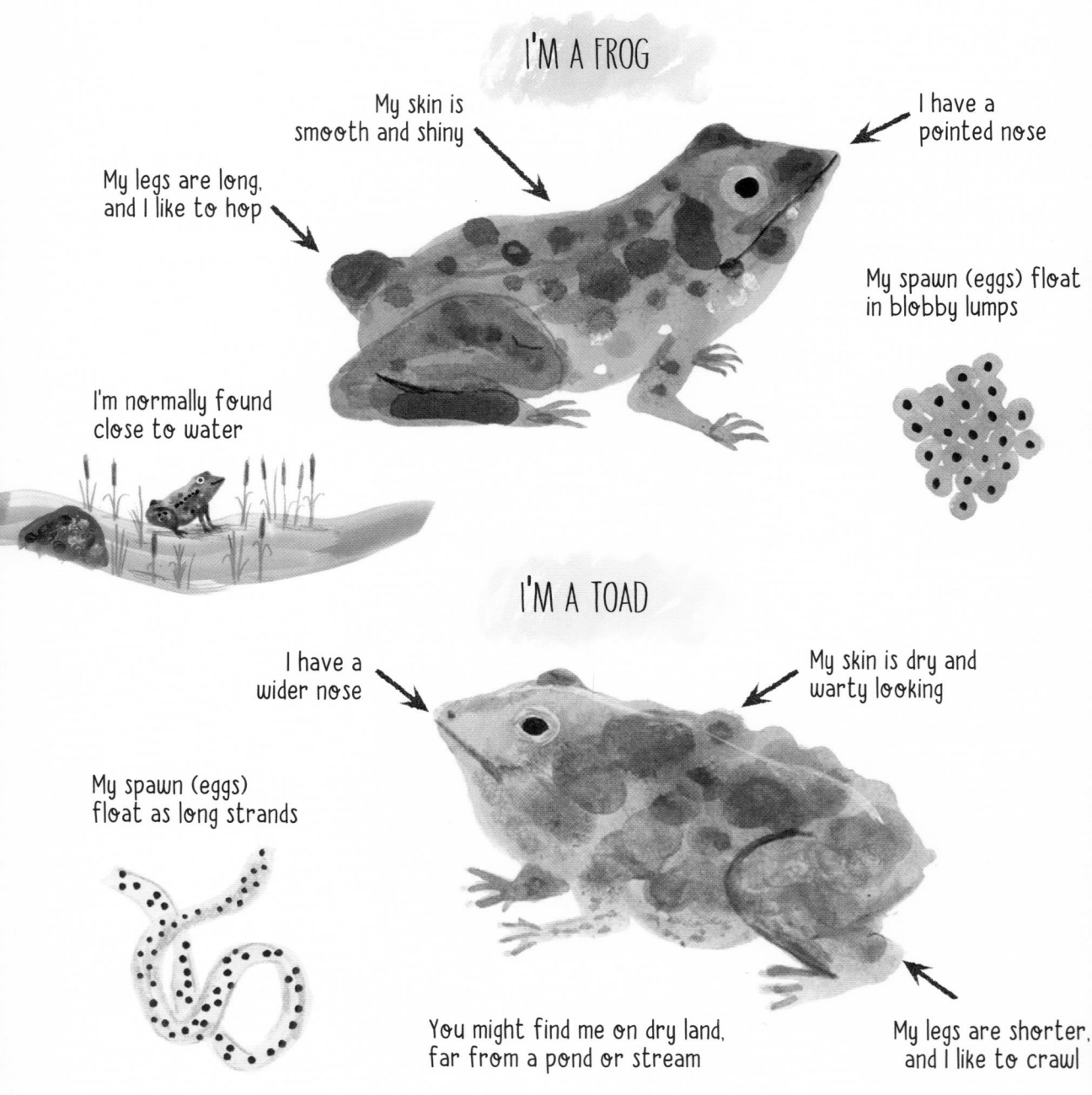

I'M A FROG

My skin is
smooth and shiny

I have a
pointed nose

My legs are long,
and I like to hop

My spawn (eggs) float
in blobby lumps

I'm normally found
close to water

I'M A TOAD

I have a
wider nose

My skin is dry and
warty looking

My spawn (eggs)
float as long strands

You might find me on dry land,
far from a pond or stream

My legs are shorter,
and I like to crawl

THE ANT

MY child, ob-serve the use-ful Ant,
How hard she works each day.
She works as hard as ad-a-mant
(That's very hard, they say).
She has no time to gal-li-vant;
She has no time to play.
Let Fido chase his tail all day;
Let Kitty play at tag:
She has no time to throw a-way,
She has no tail to wag.
She scurries round from morn till night;
She ne-ver, ne-ver sleeps;
She seiz-es ev-ery-thing in sight,
And drags it home with all her might,
And all she takes she keeps.

Oliver Herford

MAKE A MINI POND

You don't need much space to make a watery home to tempt frogs, newts, dragonflies, and other pond life. Make a mini pond out of any sturdy tub and watch the wildlife come to you.

You will need
- **A sturdy container**, such as an old dishpan, an old sink (with the drain plug), or a large planter
- **Pond-liner material** (if your container isn't watertight)
- **Sand** or **gravel**
- **Rocks**
- **Oxygenating pond plants** (that are native to where you live)
- **Optional pond plants** (that are native to where you live)
- **Shovel**

1. Pick the spot where your pond will go (and ask for permission to use the space).

2. Place the container on the spot so you can see how big a hole you should dig.

3. If your container isn't watertight, line it with a sheet of pond liner.

4. In the spot you've chosen for your pond, dig a hole big enough to place your container into so that its top is level with the ground.

5. Position the container in the hole. Fill any gaps around the container with the leftover soil for a secure fit.

6. Cover the bed of your pond with a layer of gravel or sand.

7. Decorate around the edge of your pond with rocks. You could use old tiles or bricks instead.

8. Fill up your pond with water. Rainwater is best, but if you need to use tap water, leave it standing for 24 hours before adding it.

9. Add one or two oxygenating plants. If you have room, you could also add water plants that grow above the pond's surface.

10. Sit back and wait for wildlife to turn your pond into their home.

Birdbath

During dry weather, birds can get very thirsty. You can help your feathered friends by putting out a large dish of water for them to drink and bathe in. A large plant tray or an upturned garbage can lid can work well, too. Place your birdbath in an open spot where birds will be able to see any cats that might be lurking nearby. Remember to fill it up regularly and ask a grown-up to help you clean it out if it gets dirty.

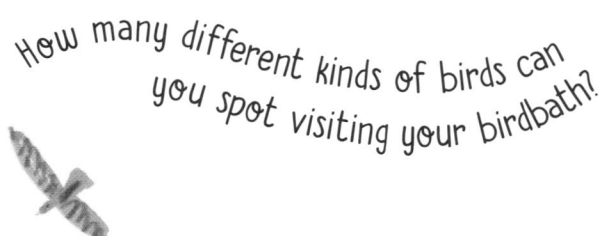

How many different kinds of birds can you spot visiting your birdbath?

Build a frog fortress

Frogs don't just need water—when winter comes, they often slow down and seek a sheltered spot to sleep through the coldest days. Build them a frog fortress to keep them safe. All you need to do is make a pile of rocks in a corner of your yard. You can also include whole or broken terracotta flowerpots to give them more places to hide. Once you've built your fortress, don't be tempted to move the rocks—you might disturb a sleeping frog.

BUILD A NEST BOX

You'll need a grown-up's help to make this nest box. If you hang it up in the right spot, a lucky bird might choose it as a safe place to lay eggs and raise her chicks.

You will need

- Plank of wood, 6 in. wide x 4 ft. 4 in. long x 0.5 in. thick (the wood should be FSC certified and not pressure-treated)
- Strip of waterproof material
- Wood glue
- Nails
- Screws
- Saw
- Hammer
- Screwdriver
- Drill (with hole cutter drill bit)
- Pencil
- Ruler

WARNING!
Using woodworking tools can be dangerous. A grown-up should be in charge at all times and do the steps that require sawing and nailing.

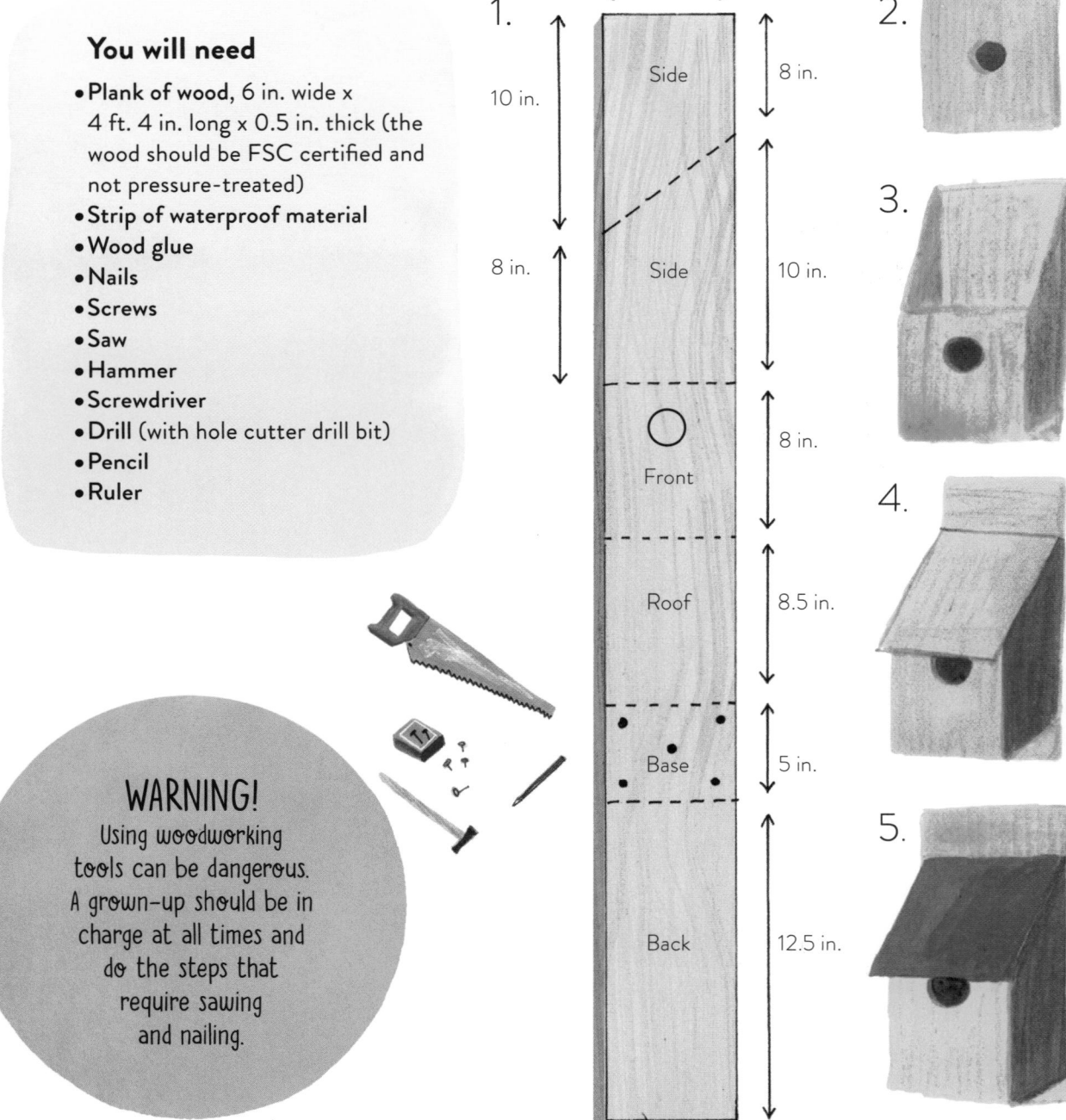

1. Measure your wood and use a pencil to mark the cutting lines, as shown in the diagram, so you don't get confused later.

2. Saw the wood along the pencil lines. Drill small holes in the base and a 1.25 inch round hole in the front piece.

3. Nail all the pieces together, except the roof piece. The back, front, and sides should fit around the outside edges of the base piece.

4. Attach the roof using screws, so you can unscrew it and lift the lid to clean out the box at the end of the nesting season.

5. Glue on a piece of waterproof material (such as rubber or roof shingle) so that rainwater won't leak into the nest box.

6. Drill holes in the top and bottom of the back piece, and ask an adult to carefully hang in the place you have decided on.

Your nest box should be placed somewhere sheltered, out of direct sunlight, and away from the reach of cats or other predators. Make sure it is attached to a wall, post, or tree trunk at least 10 feet off the ground. Don't forget to ask permission from the property owner.

ALL SORTS OF BIRD'S NESTS

You might think of a bird's nest as round and made from twigs, but different birds make different types of nests. Here are some of the main types. Keep an eye out when on your nature adventures and see if you can spot any of them!

Cup nest

A nest shaped like a cup, normally built in the branches of a tree or bush. They can be made from many materials, including twigs, grasses, leaves, moss, soft fur or cotton fluff, and even spider silk. Birds that build cup nests include blackbirds, robins, cardinals, sparrows, and hummingbirds.

Adherent nest

This is the name given to nests that stick to cliffs, caves, trees, and the eaves of buildings. They are made from the bird's sticky saliva (spit), often mixed with mud or grass. Birds that build adherent nests include swallows, house martins, swifts and swiftlets.

Pendant nest

These beautiful nests are woven from grasses and hang from tree branches. Birds that build pendant nests include weaver birds and orioles.

Platform nest

These nests are big, bulky, and built high up in trees or on cliffs. They are made from sticks and are often used year after year. Birds that build platform nests include eagles, hawks, storks, and herons.

Ground nest

You can probably tell where you might spot one of these nests. They are made from a mound of material laid down on a shallow hole in the ground—some birds use twigs, while others use soft grass or leaves, mud, or even rocks. Birds that build ground nests include swans, flamingos, malleefowl, and penguins.

Other nests

You might not realize a nest is a nest unless you spot a bird going in and out of it. Some birds, such as woodpeckers, make their nests in holes in trees. Others, such as burrowing owls, use holes in the ground. So next time you spot a hole, just think—it might be a tiny home!

BE A NATURE TRACKER

After you've set up your home for nature, you'll start to notice more wildlife coming your way. But how do you know if there are any shy creatures passing by while you're not looking? You'll need to become a nature tracker!

Whose tracks?
Look out for footprints in soft mud or snow. You will spot different tracks depending on whether you're in the country or a town. The types of tracks you see will also depend on what part of the world you're in.

Bird

Dog

Rabbit

Deer

Fox

Duck

Horse

Bear

Wild boar

Opossum

Wombat

Raccoon

If you aren't sure what creature the footprint belongs to, take a photo of it. You could ask a grown-up to help you identify it by researching animal tracks online.

Other signs to look out for

If you spot any of these, it's a sign that wildlife was in the area:

Fur

A tuft of fur caught on low branches or fences could be from a rabbit, fox, or deer.

Animal poop

Small, round droppings could be from a rabbit. Bigger ones belong to bigger animals!

Owl pellets

Owls cough up these pellets after a meal, so they are often found at the base of a tree. They contain the tiny bones and fur of the creatures the owl ate (often mice).

Feathers

These are a telltale sign that a bird has been nearby.

Nibbled nutshells

Nibbled nutshells mean squirrels have likely been having a feast.

Pathways

You might notice a little pathway worn down through longer grass. It could be the sign of a fox making its way through the area.

FEEDING NATURE

Even though we don't eat quite the same
things as the animals and insects that live near
us, we can still help them get the food they
need. After all, we humans take up so much space
with our big buildings, wide roads, and giant fences
that we don't leave other creatures a lot of space
to find their own dinner! Let's find out some
ways we can feed nature.

A FEAST FOR NATURE

The best way to feed nature is to grow plants that animals like to eat. Flowering plants will attract butterflies, bees, and other pollinating insects. Trees and shrubs will attract squirrels and birds. Birds and frogs will be drawn by the creepy-crawlies living among the plants.

Blow a dandelion puff

When was the last time you blew a white dandelion puff and made a wish? Dandelions aren't just known for being lucky—they are also food for bees and butterflies. When you blow the fluffy seeds into the air, they float away like tiny parachutes and settle on a new patch of land to grow into new flowers. If you have a yard, ask your parents to let it grow so the dandelions have a chance to flower.

Grow a wildflower meadow

However small a patch of ground you have, there's room for wildflowers. The best kinds of wildflowers to grow are those that are native to where you live. That means they have naturally adapted to live there, rather than sown from another part of the world. Fall is the best time to sow wildflowers.

What you need:
- Shovel
- Wildflower meadow seed mix
- Black plastic sheet (optional)

WARNING!
Do not spray pesticides on your garden to stop insects, slugs, and snails from nibbling the plants. Pesticides do a lot of harm to all kinds of wildlife, not just the "pests." If you know any grown-ups who use pesticides, ask them politely to stop.

1. Choose a sunny area of grass or an empty flower bed. (Don't forget to ask for permission!) The more space you have for your meadow, the better.

2. If you're planting the meadow where there is grass, you will need to dig up the turf. You'll probably need a strong adult to help with this part.

3. Pull up any weeds, and dig and turn the soil over until it is fine, with no big clumps.

4. To keep any more weeds from growing, cover the soil with black plastic and leave it for a few weeks.

5. Sow your wildflower seed mix evenly, following the instructions on the packet.

6. Water the area regularly, keeping it moist while the young meadow grows.

WHAT ARE POLLINATORS?

Pollinators are animals such as insects, birds, and bats that go from flower to flower, feeding on nectar or pollen. In doing so, they carry the pollen from one flower and rub it off on another. When this happens between the same types of flowers, it "pollinates" the flower, meaning the flower can grow fruit and seeds that will grow into new plants.

How does a bee pollinate a plant?
Honeybees collect nectar and pollen from plants to feed the rest of their bee colony and store it as honey.

1. The bee visits a flower to collect pollen. Some of the pollen sticks to the bee's fuzzy body.

2. The bee flies away to another flower to collect more pollen.

Pollen

Stigma

Ovary

Stamen (the anther and filament together make the stamen)

3. The pollen from the first flower rubs off onto the new flower's stigma.

4. The pollen travels down through the stigma and fertilizes the "egg" inside the flower's ovary. The fertilized egg grows into a seed, ready to grow into a new plant.

Why is pollination important?

Without pollination, many of the world's plants couldn't grow, and the animals that rely on them couldn't survive. We humans need insects to pollinate our crops—otherwise we wouldn't be able to grow enough food. Many pollinators are in danger because humans have destroyed their habitats (where they live) and have killed them with pesticides. Pollinators need our help!

Save a bee's life

If you spot a bee on the ground or on a windowsill and it doesn't seem to want to fly away, it might need your help! It may not have been able to find enough nectar-filled flowers and needs an urgent energy boost. Mix a little sugar and water together in a spoon or a bottle cap and put it close enough to the bee so that it can drink the sugary syrup.

Be careful not to touch the bee, in case you get stung. Once the bee has had a drink, it should feel well enough to fly away.

A BANQUET FOR BEES

The best way to help bees and other pollinating insects it to plant a variety of flowers throughout the spring, summer, and fall. Whether you have a yard, a balcony, or just a windowsill, you can do your part to provide a flowery feast.

Winter heather
This plant will flower early in the year, so it's great for feeding bees and other insects before other flowers bloom. It also likes shady areas, so it's a good choice if you don't have a lot of sunny space.

Cornflowers
These flower for a long time and feed many different types of insects.

These are just a few of the insect-friendly plants you can grow. Ask the people who work at your local garden center for their advice on which flowering plants will grow best where you live.

Lavender
Bees love lavender. The plant likes to grow in a sunny spot, and it will grow year after year. It also smells great!

Crocus
These little flowers burst up through the ground in the spring, giving an early boost to hungry insects.

How to plant seeds in pots

1. Fill a flowerpot with potting soil. Use a pot with holes in the bottom so water can drain out.

2. Look at the instructions on the seed packet to find out how deep and close together to plant the seeds.

3. Place the seeds on the potting soil and cover with a layer of more potting soil.

4. Give your seeds a sprinkle of water —don't drown them!

5. Place your pot in a warm, sunny spot and check regularly that the soil is slightly damp to the touch. Water your pot if the soil is becoming dry.

6. After a few days or a week, seedlings should appear. The seed packet will tell you how long you'll need to wait.

Sunflowers

These bold beauties are great for bees and are fun to grow. See who can grow the tallest flower!

Cosmos

This plant is easy to grow from seed and produces lots of insect-friendly flowers from late summer to fall.

Chives

Chives are easy to grow, and bees love the flowers. You can also chop up the thin, oniony leaves to season your food.

MAKE YOUR OWN BIRD FEEDERS

Birds appreciate an extra helping hand during the cold winters when food is harder to find. In the spring and summer, a bird feeder can also provide some extra food, especially helping birds feed their chicks. Here are four easy bird feeders you can make to help them through tough times.

Pine cone feeder

You will need
- Empty plastic bottle
- Birdseed or peanuts
- String or garden wire

Bottle feeder

1. Ask an adult to poke two small holes near the top of your bottle, one on each side, and a few small holes in the base of the bottle. (These are for drainage so the seeds don't get soggy and moldy.)

2. Ask an adult to help you cut a hole in the side of the bottle, big enough for a bird to get in. It shouldn't be too close to the bottom of the bottle or all your bird food will fall out.

3. Thread string or garden wire through the holes at the top of the bottle and tie the ends together so the feeder can be hung on a branch.

4. Fill the feeder with birdseed or peanuts up to the entrance hole, and hang it in a safe, sheltered place.

You will need
- Pine cones
- Lard (can be animal fat or vegetarian)
- Birdseed
- Peanuts
- String

Pine cone feeder

1. Tie a piece of string around your pine cone. The string should be long enough for you to tie it to a branch where the birds will feed.

2. Mix the lard, birdseed, and peanuts together in a bowl, using your fingers. To make it easier to mix, let the lard warm up to room temperature.

3. Squish the sticky mixture into all the gaps in the pine cone so that it is coated all over. Put it in the refrigerator for about an hour to set.

4. Tie your feeder outside, somewhere that birds will feel safe to visit, such as on a tree branch.

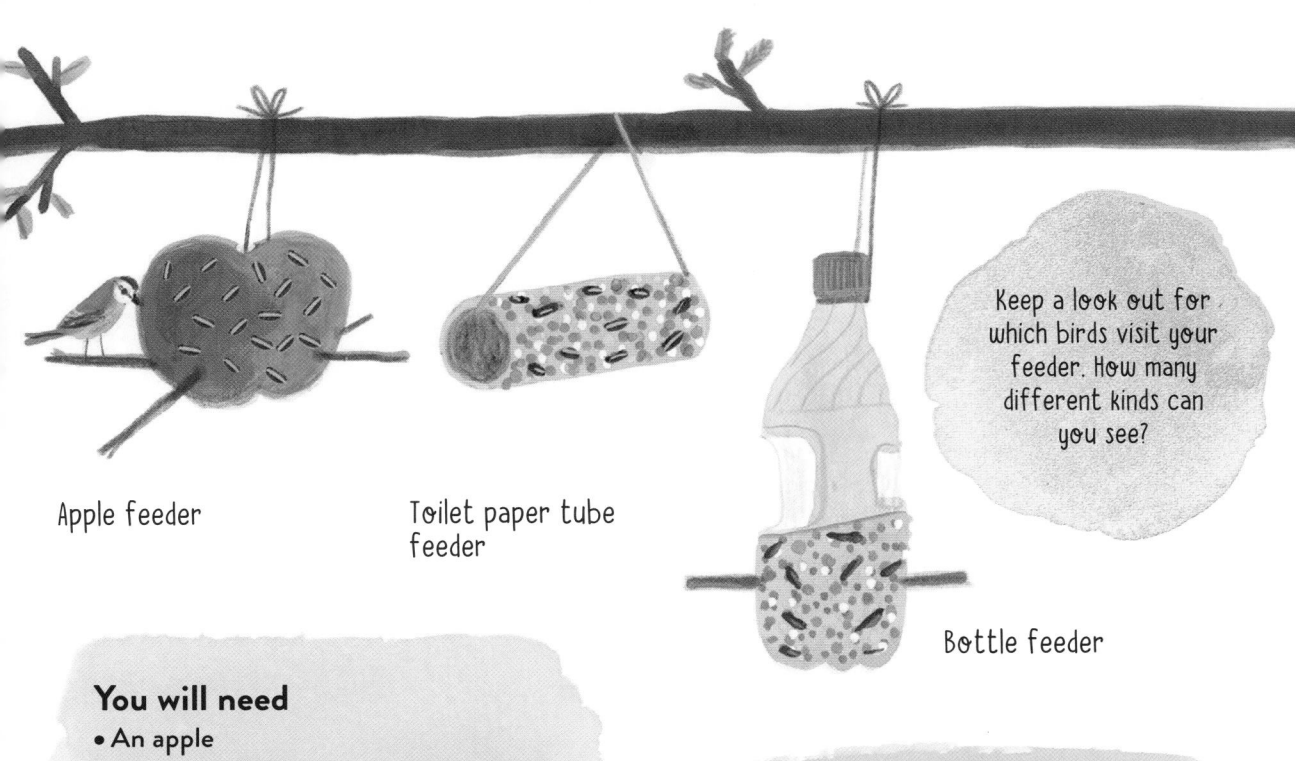

Apple feeder

Toilet paper tube feeder

Keep a look out for which birds visit your feeder. How many different kinds can you see?

Bottle feeder

You will need
- An apple
- Sunflower seeds
- Two sticks, chopsticks, or old pencils
- String

Apple feeder

1. Ask an adult to help you cut out the core of the apple. It's easier to use a corer if you have one.

2. Push the two sticks through the sides of the apple to make perches for the birds to stand on. Be careful, because the sticks can be sharp. Ask an adult to help if you are finding it difficult.

3. Press the sunflower seeds into the apple. If you like, you can arrange them in a pattern for extra decoration.

4. Thread the string through the hole in the apple and tie a knot at the end. Hang the apple up on a tree branch.

You will need
- Cardboard toilet paper tube
- Peanut butter
- Birdseed
- String

Toilet paper tube feeder

1. Spread peanut butter evenly all over your toilet paper tube.

2. Spread the birdseed on a plate or cookie sheet and roll the toilet paper tube in the mix so that the seeds stick to the peanut butter.

3. Thread a length of string through the middle of the toilet paper tube and tie the two ends together to form a loop.

4. Hang the feeder on a branch and watch the birds visit for a tasty treat!

HOW ANIMALS SURVIVE THE WINTER

Different animals cope with the cold, dark winter months in different ways. You might still see some animals out gathering food, while others will be tucked away or will have traveled to a warmer part of the world.

Adapting to winter

Some animals, such as squirrels, stay active throughout the winter. They might store up fat to have energy to drawn on, or they might grow a thicker, bushier coat of fur to stay warm. In snowy climates, the fur of some animals, such as foxes and hares, turns white to blend in with the snow.

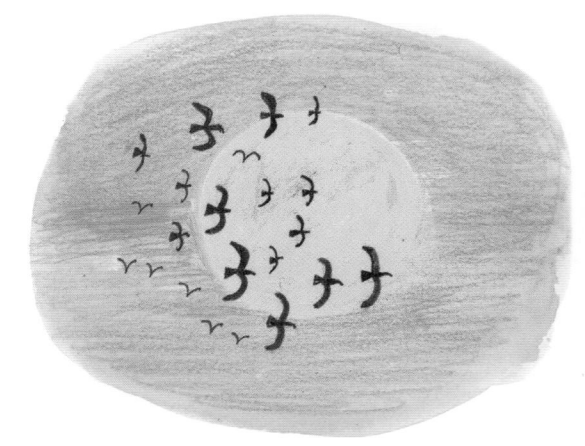

Hibernating through winter

Some mammals, birds, amphibians, and insects sleep through winter. When an animal sleeps for months at a time, slowing its heart rate and other bodily functions down, it is known as hibernation. Hedgehogs burrow into a thick nest of leaves in a sheltered place to hibernate.

Migrating to warmer places

Many birds fly south for the winter—to warmer lands with plenty of food to eat—and then return in spring. They can fly thousands of miles each year. They have a built-in instinct to migrate. Scientists think they find their way by detecting Earth's magnetic field, as well as using the Sun as a compass and following their other senses.

BIRD OF THE SKY

Bird of the sky,
How does it feel to dart and fly,
How does it feel to soar all day
"Over the hills and far away"?
To live in a tree,
To build a house as fine as can be,
To build it safe, and warm, and high,
And call it home—bird of the sky?
To perch and sing,
Up there where the leaves are quivering,
Singing and winging and building high,
How does it feel—bird of the sky?

Annette Wynne

RESPECTING NATURE

If we want to be a good friend to nature, it is
not enough to make space for wildlife and provide food.
We also have to think about the best ways of taking
care of the natural world, even when that might not be
all that fun for us. Just like we don't snatch things that
belong to our friends or push them out of the way to get
where we want, we must respect nature
and learn how to protect it.

LEAVE NO TRACE

"Leave No Trace" is a set of principles that we should all follow. Sticking to these ideas means everyone is able to enjoy spending time outdoors without harming wildlife, damaging the environment, or ruining other people's experience of nature.

Plan ahead and prepare
Know where you are going and what to expect. Bring what you'll need.

Travel and camp on durable surfaces
Stay on the trail and avoid trampling plants.
If you are camping, set up at an established site when possible.

Dispose of waste properly
Carry a plastic bag with you for trash.

Leave what you find
Don't take natural objects home.

Minimize campfire impacts
Build campfires responsibly.
For cooking, a camp stove is a good alternative.

Respect wildlife
Don't approach wild animals or feed them.

Be considerate of other visitors
Yield to other hikers and give them space.
Don't be noisy.
Keep pets under control.

Did you know that a banana peel takes two years to rot and disappear? Dropping litter or food looks ugly, can harm wildlife, and is against the law!

WHO ROBBED
THE WOODS

Who robbed the woods,
The trusting woods?
The unsuspecting trees
Brought out their burrs and mosses
His fantasy to please.
He scanned their trinkets, curious,
He grasped, he bore away.
What will the solemn hemlock,
What will the fir-tree say?

Emily Dickinson

CLEAN UP LITTER (SAFELY)

Litter spoils our enjoyment of the natural world and—even worse—it can cause a lot of harm to wildlife. You can make the world an better place and be a good friend to nature by helping clean up litter.

Where to clean up litter

- along roads (but stay on the sidewalk!)
- at the beach
- in local parks
- in the woods
- along hiking trails

You will need
- Thick, heavy-duty gloves
- A trash grabber stick
- Trash bags
- A high-visibility jacket or vest (if you'll be near roads)

Litter cleanup dos and don'ts

DO recycle any plastic bottles and aluminum cans.

DO always wear protective gloves and use a trash grabber stick.

DO wash your hands well when you're finished.

DON'T clean up litter without an adult.

DON'T pick up any sharp objects such as broken glass and needles/syringes.

DON'T pick up anything you are unsure about. Always ask an adult first.

DON'T go anywhere dangerous, such as busy roads, steep or slippery slopes, or close to fast-flowing rivers.

You can make an even bigger impact (and have more fun, too) if you clean up litter with a group of friends or as part of an organized cleanup group.

THE PROBLEM WITH PLASTIC

Plastic is a material made out of oil, a type of fossil fuel. Drilling for oil takes a lot of energy and causes pollution. We use things that are made out of plastic every day. Many of these things, such as bottles and grocery bags, are used only a few times before being thrown away.

"There is no such thing as 'away.' When we throw anything away, it must go somewhere."

Annie Leonard
Environmentalist and sustainability expert

The problem with plastic is that it takes hundreds of years to decompose, so all the plastic we throw away isn't really gone—it is filling up landfill sites (huge areas where garbage is left). Some garbage is burned instead of going to a landfill, and that causes pollution.

A lot of plastic gets washed into the ocean, where it can tangle up sea creatures or be swallowed by them, often killing them. The plastic breaks down into teeny, tiny pieces and is eaten by many creatures.

Plastic in numbers

- More than **415 million tons (300 metric tons)** of plastic are produced every year.
- **40 percent** of plastic produced is single-use plastic, such as food wrappers and bags.
- There are an estimated **5.25 trillion** pieces of plastic and microplastic in the ocean.
- **100,000 marine mammals** and **turtles** and **1 million sea birds** are killed by plastic pollution every year.

REDUCE, REUSE, RECYCLE!

There are plenty of things you can do every day to use less energy, plastic, and natural resources. If everyone makes an effort to change the way they live, together we will make a difference. How many of these things can you and your family do to help the planet?

Reduce

- Use less water. Don't leave the faucet running while brushing your teeth, and take a short shower (no longer than four minutes) instead of a bath.
- Use less electricity. Turn off light bulbs, TVs, and other electronics when you aren't using them, and ask adults to use energy-efficient light bulbs.
- Walk, ride your bike, or take public transportation instead of traveling by car whenever you can.

- Buy fewer things. Think about what you really need!
- Don't waste food. Eat up the food you have instead of throwing it in the trash can.
- Eat less meat and dairy products. It takes much more energy to keep farm animals than it does to grow crops—ask your family to try out more meat-free meals.

Reuse

- Use a refillable water bottle and lunch box.
- Use reusable shopping bags.
- Reuse scrap materials for craft projects.
- Buy second-hand clothes and toys in thrift shops instead of buying new.

Recycle

- Recycle plastic, cans, paper, and cardboard.
- Take old clothes and shoes to a clothes recycling bank. Even worn-out clothes can be recycled into new material.
- Compost food scraps.
- Make your own costumes out of clothes and scrap materials instead of buying a new costume for Halloween or other events.

Design your own "Reduce, Reuse, Recycle" poster to hang up at home to remind everyone what they can do.

"Young people, when informed and empowered, when they realize that what they do truly makes a difference, can indeed change the world."

Jane Goodall
Primatologist and conservation expert

SPEAKING OUT FOR NATURE

If somebody is mean or unfair to one of your friends, do you stand up to them? Everybody should have someone who is on their side, and nature deserves that, too! The natural world can't speak for itself, so it's our job to make sure people hear what it needs. If you think there isn't anything much that one small person can do to help, here are some ideas to change your mind.

YOUR VOICE MATTERS

However young you are, there is always something you can do to speak out for the natural world. It might seem like a challenge, but it's important that you get your voice across. To get started, why not try some of these activities?

Make a poster

Get a sheet of white paper and make a bold and colorful sign that tells people why they need to take care of nature. You could put the sign up in your window. What would your message be?

Here are some ideas:
- Reduce, reuse, recycle!
- Plastic hurts wildlife: please don't litter!
- Car trips pollute the planet. Please walk or ride your bike if you can!

Are there any other messages you want to convey? Create different signs and display them one at a time, or ask friends and family to display them, too. Don't forget to add eye-catching drawings to make people stop and notice.

Ask your school to go eco friendly

There are lots of ways your school can be a friend to nature. Tell your teacher about ideas you have for how your whole school can work together.

Maybe your school could . . .
- set up an afterschool eco club
- do more recycling
- start having "meat-free Mondays" for school lunches
- grow a nature reserve area
- grow a vegetable garden to use for school lunches and cooking classes. Your food won't have to travel!

Talk to your friends and family about why protecting nature is important and necessary. It will do a lot to spread awareness.

"The least I can do is speak out for those who cannot speak for themselves."

Jane Goodall
Primatologist and conservation expert

HELP RAISE MONEY

There are many groups around the globe that work to protect the natural world. Why not plan your own fundraiser for a cause that is important to you? You could do a challenging activity for which you collect donation pledges, raising both money and awareness.

Here are some ideas of activites you could do:

- Plan a personal runathon, walkathon, bikeathon, or swimathon for a distance you find challenging, and ask for pledges.
- Collect pledges for a litter cleanup. Can you pick up 100 pieces of litter? (This challenge helps the environment as well as raising money for charity.)

- Silence challenge: can you stay quiet for a whole day? Collect pledges!
- Drawathon: how long do you think you can draw without stopping? Ask people to pick something for you to draw in exchange for a donation.

"Surely we all have a responsibility to care for our Blue Planet. The future of humanity and, indeed, all life on Earth, now depends on us."

Sir David Attenborough
Natural history writer
and broadcaster

LEISURE

What is this life if, full of care,
We have no time to stand and stare?
No time to stand beneath the boughs,
And stare as long as sheep or cows:
No time to see, when woods we pass,
Where squirrels hide their nuts in grass:
No time to see, in broad daylight,
Streams full of stars, like skies at night:
No time to turn at Beauty's glance,
And watch her feet, how they can dance:
No time to wait till her mouth can
Enrich that smile her eyes began?
A poor life this if, full of care,
We have no time to stand and stare.

W. H. Davies

REAL-LIFE NATURE HEROES

No one can do everything to save the planet, but everyone can do something. These inspiring kids didn't wait to grow up before they tried to make a difference: they looked at what they could do to help solve problems now. Their efforts have shown they are true friends to nature.

Greta Thunberg

Swedish teenager Greta began protesting against climate change by sitting alone outside the Swedish parliament building every Friday instead of going to school. Gradually, more and more people noticed and supported her protest. Greta is now world famous for speaking up about how humans are harming the planet, and she has talked to world leaders about what needs to be done. She has inspired more than a million children around the world to protest against climate change.

"I have learned you are never too small to make a difference."

Greta Thunberg
Climate activist

Lesein Mutunkei

This teenage soccer player has a love of nature. After hearing that every day more trees were being cut down in his home country of Kenya, in Africa, he decided to do something about it. For every goal he scored, he vowed to plant a tree. He set up Trees4Goals and is planting more trees with the help of friends, family, and local schoolchildren. Do you have a hobby that you could use to help protect the environment?

Lilly Platt

This 11-year-old who lives in the Netherlands is on a mission to end plastic pollution. When she moved to the Netherlands at age seven, she began to pick up and count pieces of plastic litter with her grandfather to help her learn the new language. She was shocked by how much litter there was and the damage that the plastic would do if it washed into the ocean. Since then, Lilly has picked up an incredible 100,000 pieces of plastic. To make an even bigger change, Lilly organizes group cleanups and gives talks in schools to let others know what they can do to make a difference, too.

Amy and Ella Meek

British sisters Amy and Ella Meek set up the group Kids Against Plastic to raise awareness of plastic pollution and encourage other kids to do their part to pick up litter. They are also working to get grocery stores to stock nonplastic alternatives to single-use plastic bottles. As well as helping others take action, they have picked up more than 60,000 pieces of plastic litter—and counting.

A FRIEND IN NATURE

If you've kept to your pledge and tried the activities in this book, then you've been a pretty great friend to nature. Good job! But did you know that the friendship doesn't go just one way? If you spend time out in nature and pay attention to all the wonderful things around you, you'll begin to see that nature has a lot to give back.

When we feel stressed or anxious or sad, nature can give us a quiet space to think and be calm. When we're happy and bouncing with excitement, nature gives us space for that, too. It shows us we're just a small part of a big planet. Nature never has too many friends, and it always has time for you.

A SPACE TO THINK, A SPACE TO FEEL

Do you ever feel like there are so many feelings inside you that they need to burst out? Nature is a great listener—you can shout and whoop to let your feelings out, or you can find a quiet place to whisper your thoughts. You can sit still and watch the natural world go on around you, or explore and discover all its beauty.

"Forget not that the earth delights to feel your bare feet and the winds long to play with your hair."

Kahlil Gibran
Writer, poet, and philosopher

Nature meditation

1. Find a spot in nature where you feel calm and safe. It could be a clearing in the woods, a grassy park, or your backyard.

2. Sit down with your legs crossed, your back straight, and your arms resting by your sides. If you can't sit this way, find a position where you feel comfortable and relaxed.

3. Close your eyes and draw a deep, slow breath in through your nose. Slowly, let your breath out through your mouth. In . . . and out, in . . . and out . . .

4. As you sit, listen to the sounds of nature. What can you hear? Birds singing, the wind whistling, the leaves rustling . . . nature is all around you, and you are a part of it.

5. As you breathe, feel the fresh air filling up your chest. Think about what scents you can smell—perhaps freshly cut grass, flowers, autumn leaves, the smell of rain on dusty ground . . .

6. As you sit, imagine all your worries are butterflies, resting on your shoulders. With each deep breath, let your worries take off and flutter away.

A NIGHT IN NATURE

One of the best ways to enjoy nature is to spend time outside with your family. It's a time to talk, have fun, and watch the world go by. The longer we spend out in nature, the more we feel a part of it. So why not spend a whole night outside with some backyard camping?

Don't let a little rain scare you away from camping in your yard! It can feel very snug to be inside a dry tent, listening to the raindrops pitter-patter on the canvas.

3. Snuggle down in your bedding, keeping the tent open for now so that you can look outside. Stay quiet and still. What can you hear? What does the night smell like? Have any nighttime animals come out? Is the Moon out tonight?

4. After you zip up your tent, ready to go to sleep, can you list all your favorite things about being outside? Take turns and see how many you can think of.

1. Put up your tent together, and add sleeping pads and sleeping bags or snuggly comforters and blankets. It can get cold outside at night! Don't forget to bring a flashlight.

2. If you have a camp stove or a barbecue grill, cook your dinner outside. Do you think your food tastes different outdoors?

Top tips
If you don't have a tent of your own, ask if family members or friends have one you can borrow. It's better for the environment if we share things instead of always buying new stuff.

"No one will protect what they don't care about; and no one will care about what they have never experienced."

Sir David Attenborough
Natural history writer
and broadcaster

NATURE YOGA

Remember you are part of nature. Stretch your body with these easy nature yoga poses, and imagine you are each animal and plant as you move from one pose to the next. You should feel rested and energized. You may want to use a mat or a picnic blanket.

Seed pose
Fold yourself up small, like a seed. Imagine the energy inside you, ready to burst out into the world.

Bird pose
Stretch one leg behind you, with your arms out by your sides. Imagine you are flying into the wind, soaring far above the land.

Tree pose
Stand tall, like a tree. Balance on one leg and imagine your roots digging deep into the earth, holding you firm.

Panther pose
Down on your knees now, arch your back. Imagine you are a fierce hunter, prowling through a forest.

Snake pose
Resting your legs on the ground, keep your body upright and your arms straight. You are a sunbathing snake, tasting the air.

Wolf pose
With your arms and legs straight, lift your bottom into the air. You are a wolf stretching after a long sleep curled up in your underground den.

Frog pose
Squat down, with your hands pressed to the ground in front of you. Imagine you are an alert frog on the bank of a cool, still pond, keeping watch for a bug to catch.

Earth pose
Lie on your back with your arms and legs relaxed. Slowly, breathe in . . . and out, in . . . and out. Close your eyes and feel the breeze on your face. You are part of the earth and all that grows from it.

"I go to nature to be soothed and healed, and to have my senses put in order."

John Burroughs
Naturalist

Pick a special nature nook

With your mom, dad, grandparent, or anyone special who takes care of you, go on a hunt for a special place outdoors—in your garden, your local park, or other outdoor place you like to visit. Maybe it could be at the base of your favorite tree or a bench with a pretty view. Give this place its own special name. Come back to visit your nature nook whenever you feel like you need a quiet moment.

Enjoy the seasons

One of the best things about nature is it is always changing, just like you. Pay attention to the different sights, sounds, and smells as the seasons change. Sometimes we will feel cold and damp, but we can stomp in puddles or taste a snowflake on our tongue. Other times we will feel the warm sun and a refreshing breeze and enjoy the feeling of grass on our bare feet. Try to embrace everything that nature gives you.

Go on a worry walk

Sometimes things make us feel worried or anxious. Perhaps something has changed at school or at home and you aren't sure how to deal with it. If something is troubling you, try going on a "worry walk" with a grown-up who you can talk to. On a worry walk, we can take turns telling the other person about something that worries us. Sometimes the person you tell will be able to help think of a way to make things better. Sometimes just being able to say our worries out loud makes them feel not so bad. The great thing about a worry walk is you don't have to talk the whole time—you can just walk together and look at the nature around you.

GO

When your brain is buzzing
like one thousand bees,
Go to the trees
Go to the trees.

When your nerves are brittle
like autumn-dry leaves,
Go to the brook
Go to the brook.

When your legs want to run
like a wild, leaping hare,
Go to the fields
Go to the fields.

When your heart soars
like a bird in the air,
Go to the hills
Go to the hills.

When you're bored of your games
and there's nothing to do,
Go out the door,
Go out the door.

For Nature is waiting,
and calling for you.

Laura Knowles

FURTHER RESOURCES

National Park Service
www.nps.gov
The kids' section of the National Park Service website offers lots of activity books and guides, plus tips for parents on hiking and camping with kids. The site lists hundreds of national parks, preserves, scenic trails, recreation areas, and more—searchable by location and activity.

National Audubon Society
www.audubon.org
The National Audubon Society's website features a kids' section with activities, videos, quizzes, and more. It also includes a free guide to 800 North American birds so you can go out and start bird-watching.

Discover the Forest
discovertheforest.org
Discover the Forest is a public service campaign sponsored by the U.S. Forest Service and the Ad Council. Parents can find plenty of free resources for helping children engage with nature near home.

National Geographic Kids
kids.nationalgeographic.com
National Geographic's children's website features tons of free activities for learning about the natural world, including videos, games, quizzes, and fun facts. You'll also find in-depth information about popular animals.

Green Hour
www.thegreenhour.org
The National Wildlife Federation's Green Hour program encourages children and their parents to spend at least an hour a day exploring nature. Its website offers a selection of engaging activities grouped by season.

Below are details of the scientific studies cited on page 4:

Contact with Nature During Childhood Could Lead to Better Mental Health in Adulthood
Barcelona Institute for Global Health (ISGlobal). Published in ScienceDaily, May 21, 2019
www.sciencedaily.com/releases/2019/05/190521193735.htm
Natural Childhood
Stephen Moss, National Trust (UK), 2012
nt.global.ssl.fastly.net/documents/read-our-natural-childhood-report.pdf